Most people try to manifest by doing more.

They speak louder. Visualise harder. Repeat affirmations until their voice is flat with strain.

They've been told that energy only responds to certainty, to positivity, to relentless forward motion.

But that isn't the whole truth.

There's a missing frequency in modern manifestation —a quiet layer beneath the noise of thinking, striving, and pretending to feel good all the time.

That missing frequency… is presence.

Not the kind that's forced through meditation or rituals. But the kind that emerges when your senses are truly awake. When you notice texture. Temperature. Sound. When you begin to feel the world again — not just think about it.

This book is not about high vibes. It's not about clearing your blocks or rewriting your story. It's about remembering the part of you that already knows how to call things in.

You haven't failed to manifest. You've simply been taught to override your signal.

It's time to return to your frequency —

through Sensory Emergence™.

Sensory Emergence™

'The missing frequency in modern manifestation'

by Boz J. Levine

Founder of The Owl House

Sensory Emergence™

Copyright © 2025 Boz J Levine

All rights reserved.
No part of this publication may be copied, stored, shared, or transmitted in any form without written permission from the publisher.
This book is intended for personal reflection and does not replace medical, psychological, or therapeutic advice

About the Author

Boz is the founder of The Owl House, a private members' club dedicated to the refinement of energy, presence and quiet wealth. His work blends precision, minimalism, and sensory intelligence — offering an alternative to loud, scripted approaches to manifestation.

Sensory Emergence™ is the core of that offering: a method rooted in the five senses and the unique energetic signature of the individual, held within a Scalar field.

This book marks the first public unveiling of that method

Chapter 1

'What You Were Never Told'

Section 1 – The Manifestation Industry

They told you to think better thoughts. To repeat affirmations.

To visualise. To raise your vibration and act as if it's already done.

You've heard it in books, in courses, on podcasts and reels: "Change your thoughts, change your life."

And yet… something still doesn't quite work.

You follow the steps. You do the inner work. You stay positive, stay high-vibe — even when it's exhausting. But the results come in trickles, or not at all. You're left wondering if it's you. If you're blocked. If you're not spiritual enough. If you're failing in some invisible way.

The modern manifestation industry has become loud. It's full of bright language and bullet-point promises. And it has, in many ways, become disconnected from the body — from presence, from reality.

Most methods rely on force — even when dressed up in soft language. They ask you to override how you feel. To push yourself toward clarity, confidence, joy… even if those states aren't currently true for you.

But manifestation isn't about pretending. It's not about silencing discomfort. It's about resonance — and resonance only responds to what's real.

Section 2 – The Signal Misunderstood

The true language of manifestation isn't words. It isn't mindset.

It isn't even belief.

It's signal.

And your signal isn't something you create. It's something you already carry.

It hums quietly beneath your thoughts. It vibrates through your posture, your scent, your rhythm, the way your hand moves when you touch something you love.

It's not loud. It's not obvious. And it isn't always "positive."

But it's real. And that's what the field responds to.

When we're told to focus only on affirmations or mental clarity, we disconnect from the body — and the body *is* the broadcaster. It's where your signal lives.

This is the misunderstanding most never see. You can think abundant thoughts all day, but if your body is tense, restless, or numb — your true signal won't match the image.

And energy doesn't respond to image. It responds to resonance.

Section 3 – False Failure

This is where so many give up — not because they lack ability, but because they've been trying to manifest from a place of misalignment.

They weren't failing. They were just disconnected from the part of themselves that matters most — the part that feels.

When you force yourself to stay positive, you disconnect. When you override doubt with loud affirmations, you disconnect. When you try to visualise a life that doesn't match your current experience, you disconnect.

And in that disconnection, your signal becomes... unclear.

Not broken. Not blocked. Just distorted.

So when things don't manifest — or when they arrive but feel hollow — you blame yourself. You think you're doing something wrong. That you're too emotional. Too inconsistent. Too energetically messy.

But that's not failure. That's feedback.

The body is not resisting you. It's inviting you.

Back to slowness. Back to presence. Back to resonance — where you no longer have to pretend.

Section 4 – The Quiet Invitation

What if your sensitivity wasn't the problem? What if your emotion wasn't a block? What if the very thing you've been told to silence…is the part of you that's most capable of creating?

This is not a method that asks for performance. You don't need to prove your worth through positivity. You don't need to force gratitude or fake clarity.

You only need to become aware of the signal you already carry.

Not to change it — but to listen. To feel it.

That's where Sensory Emergence™ begins. In sensation. In quietness. In the return to what's always been there, waiting for your attention.

This is not about escaping the present. It's about using the present —as the frequency that shapes what comes next.

You haven't failed. You've simply been taught to manifest in someone else's language. Now, you are learning to speak in your own.

Chapter 2

'Awakening the Senses'

Section 1 – The Body as the Forgotten Instrument

We are taught to manifest with the mind. To visualise, to focus, to think ourselves into a new reality.

But the body is the real broadcaster. It's where your energy lives, and where your frequency becomes readable.

If the mind is a script, the body is the voice that delivers it.

When your breath is shallow, your shoulders tense, your senses dulled — no amount of affirmations can override that signal. Not because you're doing it wrong, but because you're doing it without your instrument.

The body has its own wisdom. It doesn't care if you're thinking good thoughts. It responds to what's actually happening — in the muscles, in the breath, in the field around you.

Most manifestation teachings ask you to override the body. To pretend you're calm. To imagine you're wealthy. To affirm that you're ready.

But the body knows when you're not. And until it joins you in that belief — nothing shifts.

This isn't because your body is sabotaging you. It's because it's trying to protect you. It doesn't want you to imagine a life that doesn't feel safe, or possible, or real.

It wants you to feel the truth — not force a fantasy.

When you begin to work with the body — through the senses, not against them — something changes. Your energy becomes authentic again. Subtle. But unmistakable.

Section 2 – Each Sense as a Frequency Channel

Your senses aren't just how you experience the world. They're how you communicate with it — and how it communicates with you.

Each sense opens a channel. Each one carries its own subtle code, frequency, and invitation.

Sight: What you look at shapes what you attract. Your eyes are not passive. They're transmitters. The textures, colours, light, and shapes you surround yourself with carry energy — and train your field.

Soft fabrics. Still objects. A glint of gold. Your frequency responds to everything you see.

Sound: Every sound either sharpens your field… or scatters it. Some sounds bring presence — a low hum, a bell, a breath. Others agitate, distract, or dissolve your centre.

Tuning into the right sound doesn't mean silence — it means rhythm. When you match your breath to the right rhythm, you open the body to reception.

Scent: Scent is the fastest path to memory, mood, and shift. One drop of oil can transport you into a frequency instantly — grounding, expansion, clarity, intimacy.

This is why scent is sacred in nearly every ancient tradition. Not for decoration. For signal.

Touch: Texture is language. Your body is constantly interpreting fabric, air, heat, weight.

Touch brings you into now. The right texture can dissolve overthinking. One piece of silk… a stone in your palm… the weight of a ring — these aren't props. They're anchors. Quiet conductors of energy.

Taste: Taste is the most intimate of the senses — what we allow inside.

It carries memory, identity, instinct. The temperature of a herbal infusion. The mineral sharpness of salt. The soft sweetness of honey or ripe fruit.

Taste returns us to the body with immediacy. It's not just pleasure — it's placement. It reminds us where we are, what's real, and what the moment holds.

When chosen with intention, taste becomes ritual. A sip. A pause. A small ceremony of presence.

Emotion :(The Inner Sense) And then there is feeling. Not mood, but emotional frequency. Grief. Stillness. Desire. Hesitation. Anticipation.

We're told to suppress the ones that don't sound spiritual. But every emotion carries a vibration. When acknowledged and not judged, it becomes energy you can work with.

Even sorrow has a sound. A pull. A pulse. It is not blocking you — it is calling you *in*.

Section 3 – The Energetic Field of Sensation

Every person has a field — a subtle, electromagnetic space that extends beyond the skin.

It's not just "aura" or poetic metaphor. It's real, responsive, and deeply sensory.

Your field is shaped by how you move. By how you breathe. By what you surround yourself with. And most of all... by what you feel, even before you can name it.

When your senses are awake, your field becomes coherent. Clear. Readable. Magnetic.

When your senses are numb — dulled by stress, noise, artificial light, stimulants, pressure —

your field scatters. It flickers or fades.

You become harder to read... and harder to reach.

This is why people sometimes feel unseen, unheard, or "off" — even when they're doing everything right.

It's not their mindset. It's that their field has collapsed inward.

The senses bring it back online. Not through effort — but through quiet attunement. The scent of oil. The weight of a fabric. The coolness of stone. These are not aesthetic choices. They are energetic codes.

Each sensory moment gives the body a new shape. And when the body reshapes, so does the field.

This is not theatre. It is not performance. It is natural electricity — returned to its original rhythm.

Section 4 – The Return to Embodied Awareness

When you return to the senses, you return to the body. And when you return to the body, the field responds. Quietly. Instantly. Consistently.

Manifestation doesn't require effort when your field is in resonance. What you desire begins to approach you — not because you're forcing it, but because you're available to it.

You're no longer somewhere else in your mind. You're 'here' — in your fingertips, in your breath, in your stillness.

This is where your true energy lives. And this is what

the field recognises.

It doesn't care if you're confident or ready. It responds to coherence.

And coherence begins when your body and your environment are in conversation — when the scent you choose supports your mood, the texture around you slows your breath, and your awareness touches each moment instead of rushing through it.

You don't have to force clarity. You simply have to create a space where clarity is welcome.

This is how energy begins to move. Not through strain, but through attunement.

And once you're attuned — once your signal is truly yours again — the field will do what it's always done.

It will respond.

Chapter 3

'Emergence Begins'

Section 1 – What it Means to Emerge

Emergence is not about effort. It's not a breakthrough moment, or a dramatic shift, or a grand spiritual awakening. It's quieter than that. More rooted. More real.

To emerge means to return — to come back into view after being hidden or overlooked.

This is not the beginning of a new version of you. It's the unveiling of what was always there.

You don't have to build energy. You don't have to create a persona, or perform confidence, or map out every detail of what you want.

You simply have to let your energy rise — naturally, patiently, like a tide coming in, not all at once, but undeniably. This is the difference between traditional manifestation and Sensory Emergence™.

In the old way, you visualise, you affirm, you push toward what you want. In this way, you attune — and your energy begins to gather.

It begins to shape you from within. And as you are shaped, what you desire begins to respond, not because you've chased it, but because you've matched it.

Section 2 – The Power of Subtle Energy

We live in a culture that celebrates the obvious. Loud success. Bold emotion. Grand gestures.

But energy doesn't always respond to volume. In fact, the most powerful energetic shifts often happen in silence. In the quiet adjustments. The barely noticeable refinements. The subtle changes in rhythm, breath, posture, awareness.

Subtle doesn't mean weak. It means refined. Focused. Clean.

The deeper your energy work becomes, the quieter it gets. Not because you're doing less — but because you're doing it with more precision.

Think of scent. One drop of oil can shift a room. It doesn't have to be poured. Its potency lies in how it moves — not how much is used.

The same is true of your presence. It doesn't need to be performed. It needs to be refined.

When your energy is clear and settled, you don't have to shout your desires into the universe. You simply hold the tone — and let the field respond.

That's subtle energy. It doesn't push. It pulls.

Section 3 – Resonance over Strategy

Strategy isn't wrong. But it isn't the foundation.

You can plan all you like. Set goals. Create steps. Organise, affirm, vision-board your way to the perfect result.

But if your energy doesn't match it — none of it will land the way you imagined.

Because manifestation isn't about steps. It's about signal.

And signal doesn't respond to thought. It responds to resonance.

Resonance is what happens when your body, your senses, and your environment are speaking the same language. It's when your frequency is recognisable — not because it's perfect, but because it's real.

You don't have to have everything figured out. You don't need to know exactly how it will unfold. You just need to be clear in the field — and the next step will find you.

This is why so many people burn out trying to "make it happen." They follow all the advice, all the strategies — but the field can feel the confusion. It doesn't follow effort. It follows coherence.

And coherence doesn't come from force. It comes from resonance.

Section 4 – Presence as Command

There is a point where action is no longer needed — not because you've given up, but because you've arrived.

Presence is the moment your energy stops searching. It no longer looks forward or backward. It simply holds.

And that holding becomes command.

Not in the way we're taught to command — not through force, or dominance, or intention shouted into the void. But through stillness. Through alignment. Through quiet certainty in the body.

When your senses are awake… when your signal is clean… when your space, your rhythm, and your state agree — you begin to emit a frequency that instructs the field without words.

You no longer have to reach. You don't have to "try." You become a presence that shapes its surroundings by simply existing within them — clearly.

This is not passive. It's not by-passing. It's command through coherence.

This is what emergence feels like. Not a rush of power — but the return of it. No longer scattered… no longer seeking…Simply **present**.

Chapter 4

'The Owl House Way'

Section 1 – The Philosophy Behind the Grove

The Owl House is not a spiritual method. It is not focused on health or healing. It is a lifestyle frequency — imagined, refined, and now available to those who feel it calling.

It is for those who live, or aspire to live, with quiet wealth. Not flash. Not hustle. But cultivated presence.

It speaks to a mature kind of energy — not in age alone, but in taste, in rhythm, in restraint.

Many who find The Owl House are more mature.. They are past the noise, past the grind, past the search. They are ready for a different kind of power —one that moves quietly, elegantly, and with full energetic command.

The Owl House is not about spiritual high-vibes or emotional breakthroughs. It is about environment — both sensory and energetic.

Scent. Texture. Space. Stillness used not for peace… but for influence.

This is not a place for performance. It is not curated for social media. It is a field — cultivated in private, refined over time — where wealth is not spoken of, but felt.

You won't find steps here. You'll find signal. You won't find lessons. You'll find a frequency — something that doesn't push, but quietly matches what you've always sensed was yours.

This is not a vision board. It's an atmosphere. A lived and dreamt expression of energetic elegance.

Section 2 – The Energy Room

The Energy Room is not a place filled with candles and crystals. It is an unseen chamber — precise, private, and deeply still.

Everything begins here. It's where we make the invisible available. Not to control it… but to collaborate with it.

Your personal energy is not random. It carries shape, tone, texture. It shifts according to what surrounds you — and how present you are within it.

The Energy Room isn't intuitive guesswork.

It is a sensory field — observed with care, tracked over time.

Subtle shifts are noticed. Noted. Measured.

What changes is not mood, but signal.

Each person's signal is distinct. Some are sharp and clear. Some are soft but strong.

Some have collapsed inwards from years of pressure, noise, or performance.

Our work is not to fix, but to fine-tune.

To gently restore what has been hidden —

until your energy is once again recognisable… to yourself, and to the field.

The tools are minimal. Scalar energy. Subtle crystal alignments. Stillness held with precision.

The result is clarity. And from that clarity, alignment returns. Not because we told it to — but because the environment now allows it.

This is the quiet power of The Energy Room. It is not a spectacle. It is a chamber for those who no longer need to prove anything — but are ready to shape everything.

Section 3 – The Crystal Field

The crystals used in The Owl House are not decorative. They are not mystical, spiritual tokens. They are conductors — energetic materials with precise physical properties.

Each one is selected for its resonance, not its reputation. This is not about belief. It's about effect.

Crystals don't heal you. They clarify signal. They hold tone. And when placed within an energetic field like The Energy Room, they begin to do what they're designed to do: amplify, absorb, or anchor.

Obsidian doesn't comfort. It grounds. Clear Quartz doesn't calm. It carries. Citrine doesn't attract wealth. It sharpens your relationship to it.

Each member works with a small, personal set. Not a collection — a field. Your crystal field is tuned to your unique energy — quietly supporting, not interrupting.

They are not to be touched without intention. They are not scattered around the home. They are placed with purpose, activated through stillness.

This isn't crystal healing. This is subtle architecture — held in stone.

Section 4 – Rituals of Refinement

The Owl House doesn't ask for discipline. It asks for design — the intentional shaping of your environment, your movement, and your presence.

Ritual here is not spiritual. It is sensory. It is how you create a field that supports energy without having to chase it.

You don't need incense. You need consistency. A signature scent.

A particular glass. A fabric you wear only when in alignment.

Refinement begins with the small things. A sound you always use to begin your day. An oil that immediately slows your breath. The texture of a stone in your palm as you pause before responding.

These are not routines. They are anchors. Familiar signals that quietly train the field to respond — without force, without noise.

The point is not to be perfect. The point is to be clear. To remove what is random. To reduce static. To replace it with rhythm, tone, and personal symbolism.

This is how you begin to live within your energy — not perform it. This is how wealth is practised long before it arrives.

Not through vision boards. Through taste. Through scent. Through quality.

Refinement is not an aesthetic. It is a frequency — and those who live in it are recognised long before they speak.

Chapter 5

'Designing with Energy'

Section 1 – You're Already Shaping the Field

You are already designing with energy. You just may not be doing it consciously.

Every space you walk through... every scent in your home... every object on your table — it's all signaling something. Not just to others — to your field.

You're constantly broadcasting and receiving. Your environment is not neutral. It's either reinforcing your signal... or weakening it.

What surrounds you becomes part of your tone. It's not just what you wear. It's what you see when you wake. It's the weight of the cup you hold. The feeling of the room you work in. The sound that opens your day.

Design doesn't mean minimalism or money. It means intention.

Are your surroundings lifting your energy into clarity? Or are they subtly interrupting your signal?

You don't need to change your surroundings.

You just need to become aware of how they affect your signal.

Then, with small sensory cues — a chosen scent, a softer light, a deliberate pause —

you begin to shape the field in quiet, elegant ways.

That's how you begin to design with energy. Not all at once — but with presence.

Section 2 – The Three Zones: Body, Home and Time.

There are three places you spend your life: in your body, in your space, and in time.

Each one holds a kind of tone. You don't have to fix them. But you do need to feel what they're doing to your energy.

Your Body

How you sit. How you walk into a room. The weight of your hand when you rest it on a table.

These are not habits. They're signals. Your body is always speaking — to your field, to your future, to the way the world reads you.

Soften the pace. Notice tension. Not to improve yourself — but to feel your own atmosphere.

Your Space

You don't need a new home. You need a few quiet signals that say: 'This space belongs to someone who knows what they want.'

That could be a scent. A single surface you always keep clear. A light you only switch on when you're ready to focus.

It doesn't matter how much or how little. What matters is that you chose it — with intention.

The field will feel it before you do.

Your Time

If your days are filled with noise, your energy will become hard to hear — even by you.

You don't need to organise your schedule. You need one moment that belongs to no one else.

Ten minutes. One hour. It doesn't matter how small — as long as it's protected.

It's not about productivity. It's about signal. And the field always responds to what you protect.

Section 3 – Micro-Rituals of Influence

Big change doesn't start with big steps. It begins with small signals — repeated gently, but deliberately.

A single drop of scent at the same hour each day. A certain cup used only when writing. The act of putting on a watch, slowly, before opening the door.

These are not routines. They're micro-rituals.

Quiet cues that remind the field — this is who I am now.

You don't need to meditate, journal, or write affirmations. You only need to recognise the energy of certain gestures… and begin to use them with purpose.

Examples might include:

- Lighting the same scent only when working on your future
- Wearing one specific ring or fabric when you wish to hold presence– Touching a chosen stone before speaking or deciding
– Placing a single glass, always the same, to begin a focused moment

These actions don't manifest your desires. They stabilise your frequency. They give the body and the field something consistent to hold onto — something that belongs to your next version, not your past.

You're not trying to become anything. You're just choosing to signal it — in small, private ways.

Over time, the field no longer reacts to the habits of your past.

It begins to respond to the clarity of what you now hold

not performed… but lived.

Chapter 6

'Signals of Wealth'

Section 1 – Wealth is a Tone, Not a Target

Wealth isn't a number. It isn't a destination. It isn't the vision-board version of gold taps and endless holidays.

It's a tone. It's how you move. How you decide. How you hold yourself in silence.

Wealth, in this context, is not about money — though money often follows. It's about energetic elegance. About being clear enough that you no longer reach — you attract.

The world feels this. The field responds to it. Not when you try to "act wealthy," but when you stop diluting your presence to match your surroundings.

This isn't about upgrading your lifestyle. It's about upgrading your signal — the one that tells the field: "I know who I am. I know what I hold. I'm no longer performing scarcity to make others comfortable."

When you speak less, slow down, wear something chosen — not expensive, but intentional — that's the tone of wealth.

When you protect your time, keep your home quieter, make fewer moves with more precision — that's the tone of wealth.

It isn't something you achieve. It's something you practise — and eventually, become.

Section 2 – The Things You Keep Around You

What you surround yourself with will eventually shape how you see yourself.

This isn't about minimalism. It's not about designer labels. It's about coherence.

Every object holds a tone. A chipped mug. A light you never liked. The clothes you reach for when you've given up.

These things are not neutral. They carry a message. And your energy listens.

Wealth doesn't ask for more. It asks for less noise. Fewer random items. More chosen ones.

You don't need to start over. You simply need to become more deliberate. The plate you always use for breakfast. The scent you keep for when the house is still. The fabric you prefer when you want to feel composed.

These aren't upgrades. They're cues.

They remind your system what kind of life it belongs to — even if the external hasn't caught up yet.

If you want to live in wealth, start by letting your space whisper it back to you.

Section 3 – Quiet Wealth in How You Move

True wealth doesn't announce itself. It doesn't need to. It's not in the outfit, or the car, or the holiday snaps.

It's in how a person moves. How they enter a room without adjusting themselves. How they pause before speaking. How they keep their attention close, not scattered.

Wealth moves slowly. Not lazily — deliberately.

It holds space, instead of filling it. It speaks in low tones and doesn't need to explain. It has nothing to prove, so it doesn't perform.

This doesn't mean acting cold, or controlling your behaviour. It means reducing friction in your presence.

People feel when someone isn't in a rush. They feel when someone chooses their words. They feel when someone's attention is not for sale.

Wealth isn't just about what you attract. It's about how much energy you no longer waste.

Start there. And your signal will begin to settle into something unmistakable — quiet, composed, and complete.

Chapter 7

'The Presence Practice'

Section 1 – Why Stillness Is Not Emptiness

Stillness is often mistaken for lack. For doing nothing. For being passive.

But stillness, in its true form, is pure signal.

No noise. No performance. Just presence.

The Presence Practice isn't about meditating, slowing your breath, or finding peace. It's about becoming detectable — to the field, and to yourself.

You don't have to sit in silence for hours.

You simply need moments where your energy is no longer distracted — but gathered.

This is not to clear your mind. It's to clarify your field.

Presence isn't peaceful. It's powerful. And the field responds to it without hesitation.

Section 2 – Creating a Personal Sensory Anchor

Presence isn't created through silence. It's created through coherence — when the senses are fully engaged and facing the same direction.

In Sensory Emergence, this doesn't mean switching off. It means switching on — all five senses, together, with purpose.

Not to relax. To stabilise.

You don't need a ritual. You need a moment where everything you see, smell, hear, taste and feel — belongs to the same intention.

That might mean: – A scent in the air – A specific fabric or object in your hand – A sound or piece of music – A taste — even subtle that reminds the body it's awake – A visual cue: a colour, a light, a symbol that anchors the scene

When these senses are aligned — even briefly — your field becomes readable. Not by others, but by you.

You're no longer scattered. You're here. And the field responds immediately to that coherence.

This is the essence of Sensory Emergence™: Not mindfulness. Not mood. But presence through full sensory activation — subtle, deliberate, embodied.

Section 3 – What Makes This Different

Most manifestation methods rely on repetition, belief, or elevated emotion.

Sensory Emergence™ does something else entirely.

It works by engaging all five senses at once, anchored by your DNA held in the Scalar Energy field. That's what forms the connection.

That's what allows the field to recognise and respond to your signal with precision.

When your scent, sound, texture, taste, and sight are chosen deliberately, and your DNA is present within the energetic field — you no longer need to hope the signal lands. It already has.

You're not visualising. You're activating. Not imagining — but transmitting.

Your thoughts don't lead the process. Your senses do.

This method is not a routine. It's not meant for daily use. It's an energetic practice, used in cycles — when clarity is strong and intention is present.

Your DNA is held within the Scalar field. The Scalar field acts as the **bridge** — carrying your signal into the ether.

The five senses deliver the message. The DNA holds the identity. The Scalar field moves it forward.

This is what makes Sensory Emergence™ not just another manifestation method — but an energetic transmission with direction, identity, and power.

Closing Chapter

'A Return to Signal'

There's nothing to chase now.

Nothing to figure out.

This was never about getting it right. It was about learning to feel when your energy became scrambled… and how to return it.

You've now been introduced to something most never hear about: A method based not on motivation or belief — but on physical signal.

Your five senses. Your DNA. Held in the Scalar field, carried into the ether.

That's your method. That's the difference.

You don't need to follow steps. You only need to notice tone. When it sharpens — when it settles — when it scatters.

That's all.

Because the field responds to how you live, not what you write down.

From here, you begin again — quietly, deliberately, not as a student…but as a presence.

The signal is already out there. Now it's simply time to let it reach you.

To Learn More

The Owl House remains a private offering — not a programme, not a course, but a living experience.

If the method shared in this book resonates with something you've long suspected to be true, you're welcome to explore further.

The Owl House is not in the public domain, therefore to request access to website or view the invitation, please email:

The-owl-house@outlook.com

Membership is by selection only. Not everyone will enter. Everyone is welcome to look —but few will be invited in.

Appendices: Companion Practices

The following pages offer optional rituals that may accompany your Sensory Emergence™ practice.

They are not part of the core method. They do not enhance or accelerate the signal. They are simply physical ways to meet the space — before, during, or after your emergence.

Some prefer to begin with silence. Some enjoy arranging textures, scents, or symbols around them. Neither is better. Both are valid.

Use these only if they support your stillness — not your effort.

Appendix I

Rituals of Sensory Emergence™

These are not routines. They are arrangements of energy — small, deliberate setups that allow your field to come forward without instruction.

They are not required. But for some, they provide a sensory frame that holds the signal steady.

Here are a few examples:

The Silk and the Sample

Place your DNA sample (such as a nail clipping) in a silk-lined vessel, accompanied by a single clear quartz point.

Rest it within a quiet space — preferably near natural elements: wood, stone, or plant matter.

Leave it undisturbed for a full sleep cycle.

The Five-Note Room

Choose one texture, one scent, one visual cue (e.g., candle or image), one ambient sound, and one taste (e.g. herbal tea or infused water).

Arrange these around you deliberately.

Sit with them in silence. Let the signal stabilise.

The Unseen Exit

When closing the day, light no candles. Play no music.

Simply remove one object from the space — a flower, a crystal, a glass — and say nothing.

That exit is felt. Not named.

Appendix II

Notes from the Founder

When I speak of signal, I don't mean clarity of speech or mood. I mean tone. Energetic tone — the quiet frequency that forms when the five senses are engaged, and nothing is being performed.

I didn't create this method to fix anything. I created it to reveal what was already there — but being drowned by effort.

My own practice is not complicated. It changes often. But what stays constant is that I do it alone, in a room with no mirror, no mantra, and no need to ask the field for anything.

I just let it read me.

And I trust that's enough.

— Boz

Appendix III

Crystals & Frequencies

A Refined Reference

Not chosen for their metaphysical claims, but for their sensory resonance within the field:

Amethyst — Calms energetic static. A stone of inner filtering.

Rose Quartz — Softens brittle signals. Allows beauty in.

Obsidian — Grounds the field. Carries density without distortion.

Citrine — Energises intention. Sharpens tone.

Clear Quartz — Clarifies frequency. Neutral carrier.

Tiger Eye — Adds courage to coherence. Anchors vitality.

These are not required — but they are known.

Citrine – Energy of Uplift and Movement

Citrine tends to bring a sense of clarity and lightness. It's not about being cheerful — more about shaking off that heavy, foggy feeling when things feel slow or a bit stale.

I often notice a change in my body quite quickly when I use it. My chest opens, or I find myself breathing a little deeper without thinking about it.

You can hold it in your hand, wear it on a short chain that rests near your chest, or simply place it on your body while resting. There's no strict method — just what feels comfortable in the moment.

Try this:
Find somewhere warm and quiet to sit or lie down. If you're using a loose crystal, place it gently just above your stomach (the solar plexus). If it's on a chain, sit upright and let it rest over your midsection. Rest your hands on your lap or stomach and breathe normally.

Pay attention to how your body responds — not what you think, but what you *feel*.

Reflection Prompt:

- What part of me feels clearer or lighter after this?

- Is there something I've been pushing that might shift more easily if I gave it space?

Amber – Energy of Stability and Holding

Amber brings a sense of weight and containment. I tend to reach for it when life feels too quick or scattered — when I want to slow down, come back to myself, and get grounded.

It has a warming effect, both in temperature and energy. If I hold it for a few minutes, I usually feel more anchored — like I can sit in one place and not feel restless.

Amber works well when held in the hand, placed at the base of the spine while lying down, or worn on a cord that rests near the lower abdomen. It's especially helpful during quiet periods, before sleep, or after travel.

Try this:
Lie down and place the amber near the lower belly or even tucked into a waistband. If you're seated, hold it in one hand and rest that hand on your thigh. Breathe slowly and focus on the contact point between your body and the ground. Let yourself settle.

Reflection Prompt:

- Where do I need to slow down, even just a little?

- What part of me feels steadier after sitting with this?

Labradorite– Energy of Boundary and Containment

Labradorite often shows up when I'm feeling a bit raw or overexposed — like I've absorbed too much from others, or my focus is scattered. It doesn't block the world out, but it helps me hold my space more clearly.

It's got a cool, calming feel. When I wear it or hold it, I usually feel like I'm re-gathering my own energy rather than pushing anything away.

This crystal works well on a chain that rests on the chest, or held directly in the palm. It's also helpful to place near the neck or collarbone area while resting.

Try this:

Sit quietly with labradorite in your hand or wear it close to your throat or chest. Close your eyes and imagine your energy pulling back in toward your body — just slightly. Let it sit closer to you, without shrinking. Notice how your breathing responds.

Reflection Prompt:

- What am I holding that isn't mine?

- Where could I call my energy back without conflict?

Smoky Quartz – Energy of Release and Grounding

Smoky quartz is steadying — particularly during times of overthinking or emotional clutter. It helps bring things down — not to numb or suppress, but to let the tension drain out.

I find it most useful when I've been caught in loops or feeling too "up in my head." Holding it gives a sense of dropping into the body, especially the lower half.

Use smoky quartz during stillness — place it at the feet, hold it in both hands, or even lie with it tucked under the lower back. It's best used when you're ready to let something go, even just a little.

Try this:
Sit or lie down. Place the stone beneath your tailbone or hold it in both hands. Visualise tension moving downward — not pushed, just naturally settling. Allow gravity to help you feel more present in your lower body.

Reflection Prompt:

- What am I ready to put down, even if just for now?

- How does my body feel when I stop trying to carry everything?

Rose Quartz – Energy of Soothing and Softness

Rose quartz is most helpful when there's been tension, self-judgement, or emotional fatigue. It's gentle — not to bypass hard feelings, but to help you stay soft enough to move through them.

There's often a physical warmth when I hold this stone. It tends to calm the breath and ease any tightness in the chest or jaw.

Use it during quiet rest — placed over the heart, held gently in one hand, or worn on a short chain across the chest. I also like to rest it on the forehead during evening moments when the mind is busy but the body is tired.

Try this:
Lie back and place the rose quartz over your heart or hold it in both hands against your chest. Let your shoulders drop. Breathe in a way that feels natural. If emotion rises, stay with it. Let the warmth of the stone support rather than fix.

Reflection Prompt:

- Where have I been hard on myself lately?

- What would it feel like to soften in just one small area of my life?

Clear Quartz – Energy of Focus and Amplification

Clear quartz has a way of sharpening the moment. It doesn't bring clarity on its own, but it can amplify whatever's already happening — which is why I only use it when I'm ready to look or act clearly.

It often feels cool to the touch. When I sit with it, I find my thoughts streamline a bit, and my awareness becomes more precise.

Hold it during focused visualisation or planning. Place it between the brows or at the top of the head while lying down, or wear it when preparing for intentional action or decision-making.

Try this:
Sit upright and hold the quartz between both palms. Close your eyes and bring a single word or intention into your mind. Don't force anything — just let the stone act as a lens, quietly sharpening what's already waiting underneath.

Reflection Prompt:

- What's already clear that I've been avoiding or second-guessing?

- If I trusted my next step, what would it be?

✦ Sensory Preparation Prompts

These prompts are not daily exercises.
They are here to help you gently re-enter the sensory field in the days before your planned session.

Each one invites you to connect with a single sense, using your body as the starting point — not your thoughts or goals.

There's no right outcome. You're not trying to feel anything specific or gain insight.
Instead, you're allowing the body to become slightly more available… slightly more aware…
so that when your session begins, you are already listening.

Take your time. One prompt at a time is more than enough.

Prompt 1 – Texture as Truth

Find one natural texture in your home — wood, stone, fabric, or water.

Spend two full minutes touching it with your fingertips. Don't rush. Let your skin receive the detail. If your mind starts to wander, bring your attention back to the surface: smooth, rough, cool, warm, dry, shifting…

Notice what your body does in response — not emotionally, but physically. Do you lean in? Tense? Breathe deeper? Pull away?

Optional reflection:

- What does this texture seem to ask of me — to stay still, to move, to listen?

Prompt 2 – Sound as a Marker

Choose a natural sound around you — not music. It might be wind, birdsong, the hum of water, or even the quiet tick of something electric.

Sit for two minutes and focus only on that one sound. Let it rise and fall. Don't try to label it — just follow it. If other sounds appear, return gently to the one you chose.

Notice your body's reaction. Do you breathe differently? Do your shoulders shift? Does your mind try to speed ahead or slow down?

Optional reflection:

- What rhythm does this sound suggest for my own pace today?

Prompt 3 – Scent as a Signal

Choose one scent that feels unfamiliar or rarely used — a spice, a soap, a piece of clothing, or a natural oil.

Hold it near your nose and breathe in slowly. Stay with it for a full minute. No need to describe it — just notice the impact on your body. Any tension? Curiosity? Resistance? Stillness?

If memories or images come, let them float past. The focus is on your physical response — not what the scent *means*, but what it *does*.

Optional reflection:

- Does this scent feel like something I want to move toward… or away from?

Prompt 4 – Weight as a Message

Take an object with a noticeable weight — a stone, a bowl, a book — and place it gently on your body. Choose a location that feels right: your stomach, chest, thighs, or hands.

Sit or lie still for two minutes and simply hold the weight. Notice how your body responds. Does it settle more deeply? Resist it? Welcome the pressure or shift beneath it?

This isn't about being comforted. It's about noticing where weight belongs — and where it doesn't.

Optional reflection:

- Which part of me feels held, and which part still wants to run?

Prompt 5 – Temperature as Information

Fill one bowl with warm water and one with cool. Place your hands into the warm water first. Sit with it for a full minute. Then switch to the cool. Do this slowly — not as a test, but as a way of observing contrast.

Notice how your body responds to each. Is one more welcome than the other? Does your breath change? Do you want to linger or pull away?

This is about learning your edges through sensation — not thought.

Optional reflection:

- Did my body feel more comfortable with the warm or the cool water — and what might that tell me about what I need right now?

Prompt 6 – Light as Invitation

Choose a source of light — natural daylight, a candle, or a low lamp. Sit near it without distraction and simply observe how the light touches surfaces around you: your hands, the floor, the wall, your clothing.

Notice contrast, shadows, reflections. Keep your eyes open and relaxed. Let the light speak to your attention — does it sharpen or soften your awareness?

Don't interpret it. Just stay present and let your body respond.

Optional reflection:

- What part of me feels more awake or at ease in this light — and is that something I've been needing?

Prompt 7 – Movement as Communication

Choose a small movement — circling your wrists, rolling your shoulders, or swaying gently side to side.

Repeat the movement slowly for one minute. Keep your attention on how it feels from the inside, not how it looks. Notice where the body resists or flows. Does anything shift — your breathing, tension, energy?

Let the movement be simple, like a quiet message from the body.

Optional reflection:

- What is this movement telling me — do I need to release something, stretch something, or simply rest?

Prompt 8 – Stillness as Listening

Sit or lie somewhere comfortable, with no sound or movement for at least two minutes. No music, no guided audio — just stillness.

Close your eyes and notice what begins to rise in the quiet. Is it tension? Restlessness? Peace? You're not trying to change it — just listening to what's already there.

Stillness isn't always calming. Sometimes it shows you exactly what you've been avoiding.

Optional reflection:

- What did I become aware of when there was nothing else to focus on?

✦ Pre-Emergence Check-In

Date: _____

What part of my body feels most awake today?

What part feels dull, tight, or distant?

Is there a scent, texture, or image I keep returning to this week?

What would I like to become more open to during this session?

✦ Pre-Emergence Check-In

Date: _____

What part of my body feels most awake today?

What part feels dull, tight, or distant?

Is there a scent, texture, or image I keep returning to this week?

What would I like to become more open to during this session?

✦ Pre-Emergence Check-In

Date: _____

What part of my body feels most awake today?

What part feels dull, tight, or distant?

Is there a scent, texture, or image I keep returning to this week?

What would I like to become more open to during this session?

✦ Sensory Reflections

This space is not for journaling in the usual way.
There's no need to write full thoughts or tell stories.

These pages are here to help you observe your state — physically, emotionally, energetically — before and after your session.

Write what comes. A few words are enough. You might not even write at all, but reading the prompts may help you tune in.

Use these pages whenever something shifts, or when you feel a need to check in with yourself.

This is your own sensory record.

✦ Sensory Emergence Reflection

Date: _____

During the session...

What sensations stood out most strongly? (Heat, weight, colour, movement...)

Did any unexpected memories, emotions, or images surface?

What physical response or shift did I notice in the moment?

After the session...

What's stayed with me since the session ended?

Do I feel clearer, heavier, calmer, more energised —

or something else entirely?

What might I do differently now that I've felt this shift?

✦ Sensory Emergence Reflection

Date: _____

During the session...

What sensations stood out most strongly? (Heat, weight, colour, movement...)

Did any unexpected memories, emotions, or images surface?

What physical response or shift did I notice in the moment?

After the session…

What's stayed with me since the session ended?

Do I feel clearer, heavier, calmer, more energised —
or something else entirely?

What might I do differently now that I've felt this shift?

✦ Sensory Emergence Reflection

Date: _____

During the session…

What sensations stood out most strongly? (Heat, weight, colour, movement…)

Did any unexpected memories, emotions, or images surface?

What physical response or shift did I notice in the moment?

After the session…

What's stayed with me since the session ended?

Do I feel clearer, heavier, calmer, more energised —
or something else entirely?

What might I do differently now that I've felt this shift?

✦ Sensory Emergence Reflection

Date: _____

During the session...

What sensations stood out most strongly? (Heat, weight, colour, movement...)

Did any unexpected memories, emotions, or images surface?

What physical response or shift did I notice in the moment?

After the session…

What's stayed with me since the session ended?

Do I feel clearer, heavier, calmer, more energised —
or something else entirely?

What might I do differently now that I've felt this shift?

✦ Sensory Emergence Reflection

Date: _____

During the session...

What sensations stood out most strongly? (Heat, weight, colour, movement...)

Did any unexpected memories, emotions, or images surface?

What physical response or shift did I notice in the moment?

After the session…

What's stayed with me since the session ended?

Do I feel clearer, heavier, calmer, more energised —

or something else entirely?

What might I do differently now that I've felt this shift?

✦ Sensory Emergence Reflection

Date: _____

During the session…

What sensations stood out most strongly? (Heat, weight, colour, movement…)

Did any unexpected memories, emotions, or images surface?

What physical response or shift did I notice in the moment?

After the session...

What's stayed with me since the session ended?

Do I feel clearer, heavier, calmer, more energised —
or something else entirely?

What might I do differently now that I've felt this shift?

✦ A Quiet Invitation

If something in you has begun to stir —
not loudly, but gently…
then you may already be sensing what comes next.

The Owl House is a private space.
Not a method, not a membership — a field.
It is not found through urgency, but through resonance.

If the time is right,
you'll know where to find the door.

The-owl-house@outlook.com

✦ Thank You

Thank you for stepping into this work.

Sensory Emergence is not a method to master —
it's a way of listening more closely to the body you already live in.
A return to what's been quietly waiting underneath the noise.

This is the beginning of something new —
a quieter path to wealth, presence, and refinement.
May it lead you somewhere you didn't expect,
but always needed.

— *Boz*
Founder of The Owl House

✦ Notes

You may use the pages that follow to record moments, impressions, or changes —
nothing formal, just anything that wants to be written down.